THERE'S A T.REX IN TOWN

Aleksei Bitskoff & Ruth Symons

QEB

QEB Publishing

Design: Duck Egg Blue
Managing Editor: Victoria Garrard
Design Manager: Anna Lubecka
Dinosaur Expert: Chris Jarvis

First published in the United States by
QEB Publishing, Inc.
3 Wrigley, Suite A
Irvine, CA 92618

www.qed-publishing.co.uk

A CIP record for this book is available from the Library of Congress.

ISBN 978 1 60992 590 1

Printed in China

Tyrannosaurus rex was a huge, meat-eating dinosaur.

He lived about 70 million years ago—millions of years before the first humans appeared.

But just imagine if Tyrannosaurus rex was alive today! Would he fit in with humans?

What if T. rex was kept as a pet?

A baby T. rex would make a great pet.

Small, soft and feathery, he would even fit through a cat flap.

But in just a few years, T. rex would be far too **big** to fit in the house!

What if T. rex went to the park?

Would he wag his tail if I threw him a Frisbee?

Yes, but not just because he's happy.

T. rex had to wag his tail when he ran
because his running muscles
were all inside his . . .

big, thick tail.

What if T. rex tried P.E.?

His tiny arms would be
far too short
to do a handstand.

T. rex was pretty fast on his feet.
At a speed of . . .

26 feet per second, . . .

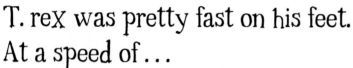

he'd be almost
5 times faster
than a child.

T. rex would be great at weight lifting! He could lift 530 pounds, or

2 large men!

What if T. rex was...
reaaaallly hungry?

T. rex could gulp down about 550 pounds of meat in one mouthful.

That's about 2,000 hamburgers!

What if T. rex came for a sleepover?
Would he pack a toothbrush?

T. rex wouldn't need
to brush his teeth.

He grew new teeth when his
old ones fell out.

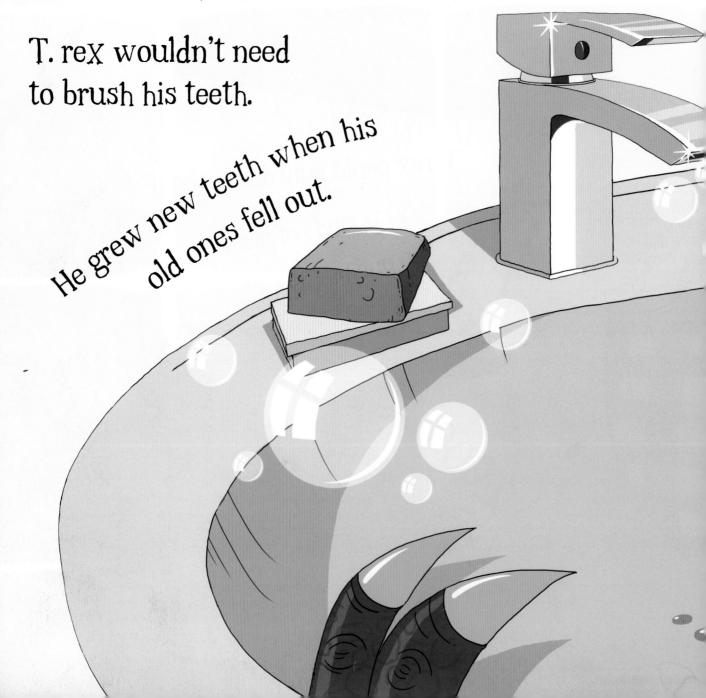

Some of them were as big as

bananas!

Would T. rex need to wear glasses?

No. T. rex had excellent eyesight. It was much better than any human's!

Like an eagle today, T. rex could see a rabbit from 3 miles away—that's the length of

500 buses lined up!

But T. rex would be easy to find...

There aren't many places

big enough

to hide a dinosaur!

Could T. rex help with recycling?

With his **big** feet and **STRONG** jaws, T. rex would be great at **crushing** cans.

T. rex had the strongest **bite** of any land animal ever!

But make sure T. rex
understands what he's
supposed to do!

What if T. rex wanted
to play the recorder?

He would find it difficult with just

two fingers

on each hand.

But T. rex would be great at playing the drums.

Bang bang bang bang!

T. rex's skeleton

Everything we know about T. rex comes from fossils—skeletons that have been in the ground for thousands and thousands of years.

Scientists can look at fossils to figure out how dinosaurs lived in the past.

This means that we know a lot about dinosaurs, even though no one has ever seen one!

X-RAY 1192289776981-789

MODEL No.: nx110005206 19571862387

hip bone

big, thick tail

long, strong legs

WYOMING, U.S.A.

Most complete T. rex skeleton found, nicknamed "Sue"—2001

ALBERTA, CANADA
Fossil found—1980

SASKATCHEWAN, CANADA—1991
Fossil skeleton found, nicknamed "Scotty"

MONTANA, U.S.A.—1902
Partial T. rex skull discovered

NEW MEXICO, U.S.A.
T. rex footprint found—1983

COLORADO, U.S.A.
T. rex teeth found—1874

WYOMING, U.S.A.
First T. rex fossil found—1900

PASSPORT

Tyrannosaurus reX

(TIE-RAN-O-SOAR-US REX)

NAME MEANS "TYRANT LIZARD KING"

WEIGHT 6.6 TONS

LENGTH 39 FEET

HEIGHT 13 FEET

HABITAT FOREST, WOODLANDS

DIET LARGE ANIMALS

23487635692003238734

T<REX<<TYRANNOSAURUS<<<<<<<<<<<<<<<<34263954302375<<<<<<<<<<<<48273526291083546>>>>>>>>